**DATE DUE**

| | | |
|---|---|---|
| | | |
| | | |
| | | |
| | | |
| | | |
| | | |
| | | |
| | | |
| | | |
| | | |
| | | |

5536

591.52   Pope, Joyce
P              Animal Journeys

NATURE CLUB

# ANIMAL JOURNEYS

## JOYCE POPE

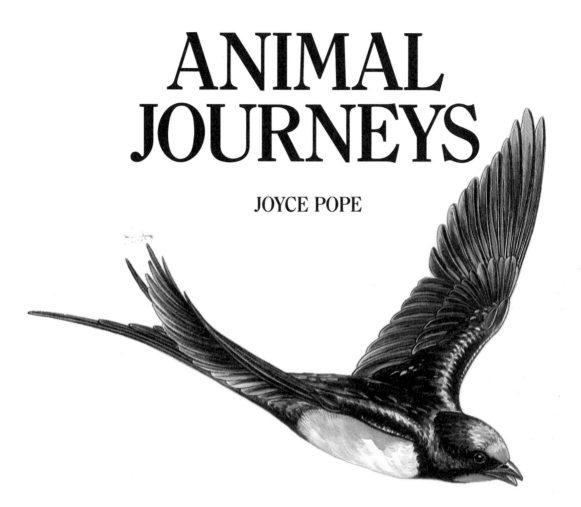

Illustrated by
## PHIL WEARE

**Troll Associates**

# Nature Club Notes

Though you may not know it, you are a member of a special club called the Nature Club. To be a member you just have to be interested in living things and want to know more about them.

Members of the Nature Club respect all living things. They look at and observe plants and animals, but do not collect or kill them. If you take a magnifying glass or a bug box with you when you go out, you will be able to see the details of even tiny plants, animals, or fossils. Also, you should always take a notebook and pencil so that you can make a drawing of anything you don't know. Don't say "But I can't draw" – even a simple sketch can help you identify your discovery later on. There are many books that can help you name the specimens you have found and tell you something about them.

Your bag should also contain a waterproof jacket and something to eat. It is silly to get cold, wet, or hungry when you go out. Always tell your parents or a responsible adult where you are going and what time you are coming back.

Unless you are lucky enough to live in a place that is on a migration route, you are not likely to see animals making their great journeys. But most people's homes are in areas visited by migrant birds and insects. Keep a migration diary in which you write down the dates that you see the first swallow, swift, or other migrants. Try to find out how many different kinds of migrants live in your part of the world. You will probably be surprised at how many there are.

*Library of Congress Cataloging-in-Publication Data*

Pope, Joyce.
    Animal journeys / by Joyce Pope ; illustrated by Phil Weare.
        p.     cm. — (Nature club)
    Includes index.
    Summary: Discusses how and why different kinds of animals migrate, the preparations they make for their journeys, and how they find their way.
    ISBN 0-8167-2777-5 (lib. bdg.)        ISBN 0-8167-2778-3 (pbk.)
    1. Animal migration—Juvenile literature. [1. Animals—
—Migration.]   I. Weare, Phil, ill.  II. Title.  III. Series.
QL754.P66  1994
591.52'5—dc20                                        91-45379

Published by Troll Associates

Designed by Cooper Wilson, London
Edited by Kate Woodhouse

Printed in the United States of America, bound in Mexico.
10  9  8  7  6  5  4  3  2  1

# Contents

Nature Club Notes                          2
Introduction                               4
How Do We Know About Animal Journeys?  6
Why Animals Migrate                        8
Types of Journeys                         10
Finding Their Way                         12
Preparing for the Journey                 16
Bird Migration                            18
Land Mammals                              20
Sea Mammals                               22
Fish                                      24
Plankton                                  26
Insects                                   28
Glossary                                  30
Index                                     31

# Introduction

One of the most important things about animals is that they are able to move from one place to another. Most animals are small creatures without backbones whose life is very brief. Some of them move about in search of food, shelter, or a mate, without going in any particular direction. They may be blown by the wind or carried by water currents, but they are not great travelers. Other animals without backbones, such as barnacles and oysters, stay in one spot for most of their lives, but even they may make long journeys when they are very young.

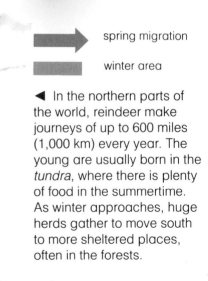

➡️ spring migration

winter area

◀ In the northern parts of the world, reindeer make journeys of up to 600 miles (1,000 km) every year. The young are usually born in the *tundra*, where there is plenty of food in the summertime. As winter approaches, huge herds gather to move south to more sheltered places, often in the forests.

◀ This map shows where reindeer in Scandinavia migrate each year. All migration journeys are perilous. Like migrants in other parts of the world, many deer die from exhaustion or hunger or are killed by people hunting them. Now reindeer face a new risk. Radioactivity from Chernobyl has damaged much of their range, but some still manage their ancient migrations.

Some creatures, such as barn owls and beavers, are known as *sedentary* animals. When they first leave their parents, they may roam long distances before they find a suitable place to live. When they have found it, they do not move away.

Other creatures may travel thousands of miles each year on regular *migrations*. Some birds, such as swallows, never know winter. They fly north for summer and then when autumn comes they return south to warmer weather in Africa or South America. These voyages are full of danger. Enemies and bad weather mean that many animals never finish their journey. Even so, these animals must attempt the trip, for they could not survive all the year in the home they make at either end of their journey.

▲ Only young beavers travel any distance. When they leave their parents they look for a suitable place to live. Then they do not move again.

▼ Adult barnacles use their legs to kick food into their mouths, not to move. Young barnacles are small and may float long distances before they find a place to settle down for the rest of their lives.

# How Do We Know About Animal Journeys?

In times when most people did not travel far from their own villages, they would have found it difficult to believe that animals made much greater journeys. The tribes who depended on animals for their food knew that the herds traveled to other places, but they did not know where they went.

▼ Most kinds of whales spend their lives traveling around the oceans. Gray whales feed in the cold seas between Alaska and Asia during the summer and breed near the warm lagoons off the coast of Mexico during the winter.

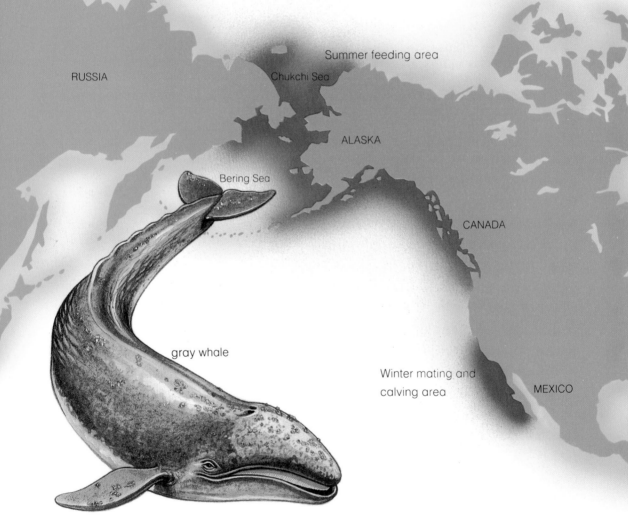

RUSSIA

Summer feeding area

Chukchi Sea

ALASKA

Bering Sea

CANADA

gray whale

Winter mating and calving area

MEXICO

monarch
butterfly

◄ Even insects, like the monarch butterfly, can be great travelers. Tagged butterflies have been recaptured far from their starting point.

▼ This curlew is ringed with a numbered metal band, so it is possible to record its journeys over many years.

curlew

Birds were the most obvious creatures that came and went in such a mysterious way. Homer, who lived about 800 B.C., was just one of the ancient writers who described the coming of birds in spring and their flight before the harshness of winter. About 450 years later, Aristotle tried to work out why this should happen. In northern Europe, people saw that cuckoos and swallows disappeared at the end of summer, but they had no idea how far these small animals could fly. They supposed that cuckoos turned into hawks and that swallows burrowed into the mud of reed beds to sleep through the winter.

Nowadays it is possible to track animals that migrate. The easiest way is to mark the animal with a distinctive tag, so that if it is found in another part of the world, it can be recognized. Tags have enabled scientists to discover many things about the distances and directions that animals travel. In recent years, the flight of birds has often been monitored on radar screens. It is also possible to attach lightweight transmitters which record the animals' wanderings.

# Why Animals Migrate

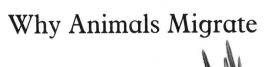

One of the
most important
reasons animals
migrate is to find food.
In parts of East Africa,
zebras and wildebeests spend
almost all of their lives in slow
migration. They move on each day
to fresh pastures and seem to know
where it has rained and where there
will be fresh grass. This migration means
they feed without overgrazing any one place.
Other mammals, such as barren-ground
caribou, migrate north in the summer to find
snow-free pastures.

Some animals migrate to avoid bad
weather. Many birds fly to warmer countries
in the winter. They go no farther than places
where the ground is unfrozen and they can
find food. Sometimes, when there is a very
hard winter, rare birds such as snowy owls are

▲ Swallows feed on flying
insects. Their young hatch
in the northern parts of the
world, where there is plenty
of food in the summertime.
In the winter, when it is too
cold for insects to survive,
the swallows fly south to
a warmer climate where
there are many insects.

seen much farther south than usual. Climate is also why many fish and whales migrate, traveling between their feeding grounds and warmer breeding grounds to have their young.

Another important reason for migration is the search for a place where there is enough space and food to raise a family. The birds that leave the tropics in the summertime spread out into a much greater area of land in the northern continents. There is room for each pair of birds to have plenty of space to raise their young. Also, the farther north you go in the summer, the longer the hours of daylight. This gives birds with hungry broods enough time to find food for them.

▼ On the great grassy plains of Africa, zebras and antelopes move a little most days, following the supply of fresh grass and leaves. In periods of drought, they may move much farther to find a place where it has rained.

▲ Sedge warblers, like swallows, feed on insects. In their northern breeding areas they find nesting places, usually close to water, where there is plenty of food.

9

# Types of Journeys

Most creatures we see are probably looking for food and are not likely to travel far. If we notice a number of animals traveling purposefully in the same direction, it is likely that they are migrating or moving from one living space to another.

One kind of movement is called *dispersal*. This happens particularly when young animals leave their parents. They strike out in almost any direction. Young gray seals have been found in Scandinavian waters as well as off the coast of Spain only fourteen days after leaving the same Scottish breeding colony. In autumn, huge numbers of waxwings move south from their far northern breeding grounds. Sometimes, after a very successful breeding season, an *irruption* of birds reaches much farther south than usual.

▲ Anna's hummingbird lives mainly in California and Mexico. It moves north in spring, to places near houses where there are plenty of flowers. Recently, it has been seen in Texas in autumn, so it may be gradually spreading beyond its old habitat.

▼ Baby gray seals stay on land and feed on their mother's rich milk until they are about four weeks old. Then they shed their white coats and swim out to sea on their own.

Many birds and mammals travel from wintering grounds in the tropics toward the north. Once their migration has started, they travel steadily, though some species stop to feed regularly along the way. Other animals, such as some hummingbirds, make short but important changes in their habitats by migrating from one zone to another up or down a mountainside. In the sea, many tiny planktonic creatures, fish, and squid make a daily migration from the depths of the ocean to the surface waters.

The distances that animals travel are often very great. The longest journeys are made by Arctic terns. These birds nest around the northern coasts of the world, but after breeding they start on a migration that takes them on a round trip of 22,000 miles (35,420 km). Some cross the Atlantic Ocean twice in the course of this marathon. Others travel down the west coast of the Americas to winter with the other birds in cool Antarctic waters.

▲ Shearwaters spend almost all of their lives at sea, only coming ashore to nest on remote headlands and islands. Most of the year they roam the oceans, sometimes traveling thousands of miles between one breeding season and the next.

► Waxwings live in northern forests. Sometimes they are driven south by severe winters. The arrival of a flock of waxwings is always an exciting event for bird watchers.

# Finding Their Way

One of the puzzles about migration is how the animals find their way. Some migrants, such as antelopes and whales, are social animals and travel in family groups. The young ones learn the route from those who have made the journey many times before. But some animals travel alone. In Europe, cuckoos leave the north soon after their eggs are laid and leave their babies to be brought up by other birds. As soon as they can fly strongly, the young birds set out alone on the long journey to Africa. The ability to do this is called *instinct* or *innate knowledge*. It means that birds are born programmed to make this journey. As an experiment, birds that hatched from eggs laid in western Europe were taken to eastern Europe. When these birds migrated, they flew in the direction that would have been the right one from their proper home.

▲ Homing and carrier pigeons will find their way home, probably because they have a natural compass in their brains.

◄ In the dry season, African elephants usually stay near water, but once the rains come they wander across large areas. They keep to the same routes each year so the young learn the way to the best shelter, food, and water.

Most animals use landmarks to help them find their way. Over short distances, they use small rivers, towns, and even trees. Landmarks on longer journeys include coastlines, mountain ranges, and valleys.

Many birds use the sun and stars to find their way. This was proved by keeping birds in a planetarium, where it is possible to alter the position of stars and planets. The birds always try to fly in the direction which would be the correct one for the "sky" they can see, even when it would take them the wrong way.

For people, the compass is one of the most important aids to navigation. The magnetic pointer always shows north, so people can check the direction in which they are traveling. Many animals have tiny crystals of a mineral called magnetite in their cells. These act as a built-in compass, so the migrants have a constant check on their direction.

▲ Geese travel long distances on migration each year, like many other water birds. Huge numbers of birds use great flyways, which follow coastlines, valleys, or mountain ranges, as they journey to and from their northern breeding grounds.

# Finding their way

Birds and large mammals are not the only creatures that need to be skillful navigators. On a smaller scale, insects such as bees and wasps must find their way back to their nests. Although their journeys are not so great, they are often quite long compared to the size of the animals. We know that some insects use landmarks. One hunting wasp that catches caterpillars for her grubs to eat climbs to the top of a plant to get a view of her surroundings. She then leaps off in the direction of her nest, flying as far as she can with her load.

Many insects have other navigational aids. Some have eyes that can detect patterns of light in the sky. A honeybee, for instance, can use polarized light patterns like a map to help find its way back to the hive. Air currents often influence the movements of insects.

▼ This caterpillar-hunting wasp may have to drag her paralyzed prey for more than 300 feet (92 m) to her nest. She recognizes landmarks from the air but needs to check her position from time to time, since she has to go around plants and stones as she hauls her heavy prey home.

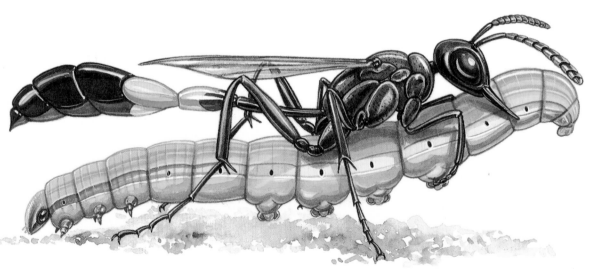

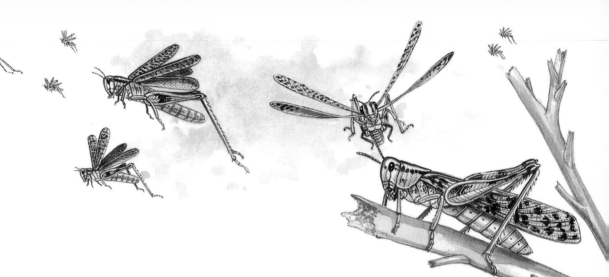

Swarms of locusts may be carried long distances by the wind. Other insects fly into the wind because they are able to find mates and food by following scents in the air.

In water, fish use currents in a similar way. Sometimes they are carried by the currents, and other times they swim across them. Sea and freshwater fish both use the sun for navigation. It has been observed that white bass, when heading for their breeding areas, become disoriented on dull or cloudy days.

▲ Locusts take off into the wind, but if the air currents strengthen, the locusts may be carried off course. Locusts are affected by the sight of other locusts flying nearby. A swarm of locusts may fly for hundreds of miles, but a solitary locust will quickly come to land.

► The eyes of a honey-bee can appreciate colors and shapes. Bees navigate by landmarks as they return to their hives after collecting nectar from flowers. They also use patterns of light that are invisible to us.

# Preparing for the Journey

Animals prepare for migration in many different ways. For some animals, it is changes in daylight length or the scarcity of food that starts them on their journey. Migrating animals also seem to have an internal clock which tells them when it is time to start to make a move. These changes, both inside and outside the animals' bodies, often make them restless. Birds in particular prepare for their long and dangerous journeys. They may need to fly for long distances over the sea, or other places where they can neither rest nor find food. This means their migration cannot begin until they have grown fat. Fat is the best sort of fuel, and some small birds nearly double their weight before they start to migrate.

▲ Young swifts begin their migration soon after they leave the nest. They can fly strongly, as they strengthen their wing muscles by beating their wings for several days before they take to the air for the first time.

▼ Some kinds of hummingbirds, such as this ruby-throated, make long migrations. After they have reared their nestlings, they eat as much as they can while food is still plentiful. They store the surplus as fat, which is fuel for their journey.

Other animals also become very fat before they start their migration. Salmon grow fat from feeding in the sea before they start their journey to their spawning streams. At the end of their journey they do not eat until they have laid their eggs. By this time they are thin and weak, and many die. Freshwater eels change before they make their great journey to the sea to spawn. They become very fat and even stop eating, losing their ability to digest food.

▼ Green turtles migrate farther than any other reptile. They sometimes travel as much as 2,000 miles (3,200 km) between their feeding grounds and the beaches where their eggs are laid. They carry a great deal of fat, for they eat little on the long journey.

# Bird Migration

Migrant birds announce the coming of summertime to people living in the Northern Hemisphere. Many species, including warblers, swallows, cuckoos, ducks, geese, waders, and sea birds, fly north from the tropics where they spend the winter. Birds of prey and cranes, who do not need the protection of darkness, fly by day. Ducks and geese fly by night or in the daylight. Most small birds that travel long distances move by night, though short-distance migrants usually fly in the early part of the day. Most migrants stop to feed and rest for a part of each day, unless they are flying over deserts or the sea.

Different kinds of birds fly at different speeds. They may be helped or hindered by strong winds, which can blow them totally off course. Small songbirds travel slowest, usually flying at less than 30 miles (48.3 km) per hour. Ducks and geese usually fly much faster.

Arctic tern

**Key**

White stork

Swallow

Bobolink

American golden plover

Arctic tern

Short-tailed shearwater

American golden plover

18

The journeys of some birds have been followed in detail. Some blue geese flew from southern Canada to Louisiana, a distance of 1,500 miles (2,415 km) in three days. Some kinds of birds have been checked, either from aircraft or by radar, flying at very great heights. The altitude record is probably held by some geese which crossed the Himalayas at over 30,000 feet (9,100 m). Cranes and other large birds often fly high, but most small species stay close to the ground and are rarely recorded above 800 feet (243 m).

Slender billed shearwater

*Woodland Presbyterian School*

# Land Mammals

The migrations of land mammals were once far greater than they are today. The reason is that people have taken over much of the earth's surface. There are now cities and farms where great herds of mammals used to roam. Only in remote areas is there still large-scale mammal migration.

In parts of Africa, particularly where there are big game parks, many kinds of antelope still make their annual migration. This varies with the weather. In seasons with plenty of rain, they do not need to travel as far as in dry periods. The barren-ground caribou of the far north travel each year from the *taiga* forests to the *tundra*, where there is plenty of food during the brief Arctic summer. They are followed by wolves that prey mostly on weak or injured animals.

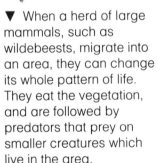

▼ When a herd of large mammals, such as wildebeests, migrate into an area, they can change its whole pattern of life. They eat the vegetation, and are followed by predators that prey on smaller creatures which live in the area.

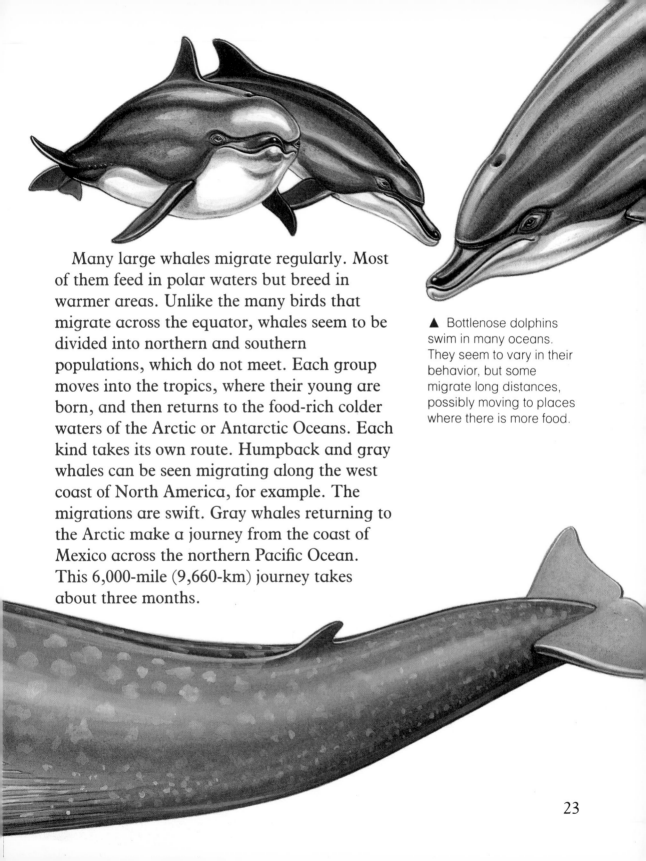

Many large whales migrate regularly. Most of them feed in polar waters but breed in warmer areas. Unlike the many birds that migrate across the equator, whales seem to be divided into northern and southern populations, which do not meet. Each group moves into the tropics, where their young are born, and then returns to the food-rich colder waters of the Arctic or Antarctic Oceans. Each kind takes its own route. Humpback and gray whales can be seen migrating along the west coast of North America, for example. The migrations are swift. Gray whales returning to the Arctic make a journey from the coast of Mexico across the northern Pacific Ocean. This 6,000-mile (9,660-km) journey takes about three months.

▲ Bottlenose dolphins swim in many oceans. They seem to vary in their behavior, but some migrate long distances, possibly moving to places where there is more food.

# Fish

Most of the fish that live in rivers and lakes occupy a particular habitat and do not move very far during their whole lives. But a few kinds, such as the whitefish in some northern lakes, migrate short distances into streams to find suitable places to spawn. In the sea many fish, including most species important as food for people, move to shallow water to lay their eggs. In the tropics young barracuda hatch and spend their early months in the warmth of mangrove swamps before taking to the open sea.

Salmon and freshwater eels make far longer journeys. These species can move from fresh to salt water, something that is impossible for most fish. Salmon hatch and spend up to five years in mountain streams. They then migrate to the sea, where they feed and grow for several years more. When they return, they

▼ Adult salmon, fat and strong from feeding in the sea, return to fresh water to breed. Their eggs and young need the cool, fast-flowing water of mountain streams. Before they reach such places, the salmon may need to fight their way through rapids or leap waterfalls. Many salmon rivers can no longer be used by the fish for they have been dammed for hydroelectricity. In some places however, salmon ladders have been built, so they can climb over the dams.

newly hatched eel

1½ years

3 years

navigate by the Sun to a stream much like the one in which they hatched, and which they recognize by its smell. Here they spawn and then they usually die. Most European salmon do not have to travel far in fresh water, but some North American species, such as the king salmon, may swim over 2,000 miles (3,220 km) before reaching their spawning grounds.

Eels are born in the sea and swim slowly in deep water to the mouths of rivers in Europe or America. They then swim upstream where they feed and grow, eventually becoming fat and silvery-colored. They return to the deep sea where they lay their eggs and die.

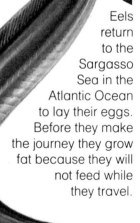

North Atlantic Ocean

Sargasso Sea

◄ Eels return to the Sargasso Sea in the Atlantic Ocean to lay their eggs. Before they make the journey they grow fat because they will not feed while they travel.

# Plankton

Plankton is a name given to many different kinds of animals and some plants that float in water, particularly those carried by sea currents. The name comes from a Greek word that means "wandering." Although some planktonic animals, such as jellyfish, are large, most are small and none can make their way against currents.

Some planktonic animals live on the surface of the water and are blown by the wind. One of the biggest is the Portuguese man-of-war, which has a gas-filled float that acts as a sail. Another is the bubble-raft snail, which hangs below the surface of the water, attached to a raft of bubbles.

▼ The air-filled bubbles of the bubble-raft snail harden soon after they are formed, so they feel like a piece of plastic.

▼ Some planktonic animals and plants change to become familiar creatures such as crabs or jellyfish. Others such as the copepod and the dinoflagellate remain small and part of the plankton group for all of their lives.

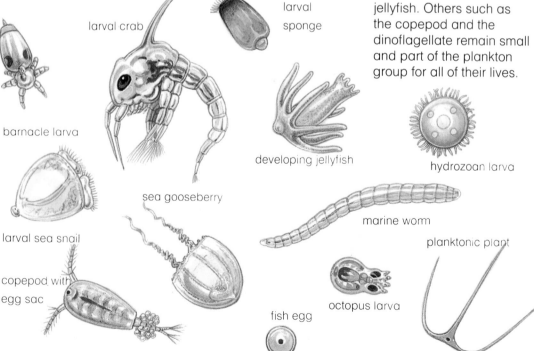

larval crab

larval sponge

barnacle larva

developing jellyfish

hydrozoan larva

larval sea snail

sea gooseberry

marine worm

planktonic plant

copepod with egg sac

fish egg

octopus larva

◄ The gas-filled floats of the Portuguese man-of-war carry its stomach and tentacles. The tentacles have powerful stinging cells which paralyze its prey.

Some planktonic animals are tiny, often too small to see without a microscope. Most of them are strangely shaped, with long spines or lobes. These help to support them in the water, like built-in water skis. Many planktonic animals are the young or larvae of creatures such as sea snails, crabs, or barnacles. As plankton, they can escape from the place in which their parents live and colonize new areas, though many of them end up as food for fish or other creatures.

One strange thing about many planktonic animals is that they make long journeys up and down in the water in the course of every 24 hours. They come to the surface at night and sink down in bright light. They are probably trying to keep in the level of light that suits them best, but nobody is sure.

# Insects

Most insects are too short-lived to complete long migrations like birds and other large animals. Yet many species, including butterflies, moths, beetles, and dragonflies do migrate, often over great distances. Like other animals, they have regular migration routes. Though they probably navigate mainly by the sun and light of the sky, they follow coastlines and valleys, just as birds do.

The difference between insect migration and bird or mammal migration is that the journey of an insect is usually a one-way trip. The return journey is made by a different generation of insects from those that set out. In spring, monarch butterflies start to fly north from their wintering grounds in California,

▲ Some ladybugs migrate to hibernating places. This American species moves into mountainous areas in late summer. It is one of the few insects that has a two-way migration, for it returns to the lowlands the next spring. In France there is a related species which feeds on aphids that infest vines. Because they are so useful, farmers put up hibernating boxes for them.

◄ The cabbage white butterfly migrates from mainland Europe to Britain each year. It has also been introduced in America. A related butterfly, the great southern white, migrates from Florida in the spring.

► Painted lady butterflies migrate long distances – some have even been known to cross the Atlantic. Nobody is quite sure why they make such journeys. They breed in their new home, but few of their offspring survive the next winter. It may be that migration prevents overpopulation in warmer areas.

▼ Some kinds of dragonflies migrate long distances, often traveling in large groups.

Texas, and Florida. The females lay eggs as they go. The butterflies that develop from these eggs stay where they are, but the migrants continue until they have reached Canada, where more eggs are laid. The insects that hatch migrate back to their hibernating places in the south.

Another butterfly that is a great traveler is the painted lady, which has been found almost all over the world. These butterflies can make long sea crossings helped by the wind, and have been seen resting on a calm sea and taking off again. It is only when the weather is rough that they get beaten into the water and drown.

The range of animals that migrate is huge, from the smallest insects to the largest whales.

# Glossary

**dispersal** the spread, in any direction, of animals that have been in a particular place, for breeding or some other purpose.

**hibernation** the coma-like sleep in which some animals pass the winter months. Their temperatures drop, their hearts beat very slowly and they breathe much less frequently than normal. They do not need to feed for they use little energy while in this state.

**innate knowledge** something, usually a pattern of behavior, that does not have to be learned. It is sometimes called *instinct*.

**irruption** an increase in the numbers of animals of a particular kind in a place where they are not usually common. Irruptions are not regular, like migrations, and are generally due to changes in the environment.

**migration** the movement, on a regular basis, of all or a large part of a population of animals from one area of the world to another. Migration journeys may be quite short but are often very long. They are made by many kinds of animals including some insects, fish, birds and mammals.

**sedentary** animals that do not migrate.

**taiga** the name given to great coniferous forests that stretch across the northern continents of the world from Europe through Asia and North America.

**transhumance** the movement of peoples who travel with their livestock to new feeding grounds at different seasons of the year.

**tundra** a zone of low-growing plants found in the most northerly parts of the northern continents of the world where the weather is very cold for most of the year. The subsoil is permanently frozen. Only the surface thaws in the summer. As a result the ground tends to be water-logged. The word tundra comes from an Inuit word meaning "treeless."

# Index

American golden plovers, *18*
antelopes, *9, 12, 20*
arctic terns, *11, 18*
Aristotle, *7*
barn owls, *5*
barnacles, *4, 5, 27*
barracudas, *24*
bats, *21*
beavers, *5*
bees, *14, 15*
beetles, *28*
birds, *7, 11, 18–19*
  irruptions, *10*
  navigation, *12, 13*
  preparation for journey, *16*
  reasons for migration, *8, 9*
  tagging, *7*
bobolinks, *18*
breeding, *9*
butterflies, *7, 28–29*
  cabbage white, *28*
  monarch, *7, 28–29*
  painted lady, *29*
  tagging, *7*
caribou, barren-ground,
  *8, 20–21*
climate, *8–9*
compasses, *12, 13*
crabs, *26, 27*
cranes, *18, 19*
cuckoos, *7, 12, 18*
curlews, *7*
dispersal, *10, 30*
dolphins, bottlenose, *23*
dragonflies, *28, 29*
ducks, *18*
eels, *17, 24–25*
elephants, *12*

fat, *16, 17*
fish, *9, 11, 15, 22, 24–25*
food, *8, 9, 10, 16*
geese, *13, 18, 19*
  blue, *19*
hawks, *7*
hibernation, *21, 30*
Homer, *7*
human beings, *21*
hummingbirds, *10, 11, 16*
  Anna's, *10*
  ruby-throated, *16*
innate knowledge, *12, 30*
insects
  as food, *8, 9, 21*
  migration, *28–29*
  navigation, *12–13, 14*
instinct, *12, 30*
irruptions, *10, 30*
jellyfish, *26*
ladybugs, *28*
landmarks, *12, 13, 14, 15*
locusts, *15*
magnetite, *13*
mammals, *20–21, 22–23*
moths, *28*
navigation, *12–13, 14*
  by stars, *13*
  by sun, *13, 15, 28*
owls, snowy, *8–9*
oysters, *4*
pigeons, *12*
plankton, *11, 22, 26–27*
polar bears, *22*
Portuguese man-of-war,
  *26, 27*
radar, *7, 19*
reindeer, *4–5, 21*

salmon, *17, 24–25*
sea
  birds, *18*
  fish, *11, 15, 24, 25*
  mammals, *22–23*
  plankton, *11, 22, 26–27*
seals, *10, 22*
  gray, *10*
  northern fur, *22*
sedentary animals, *5, 30*
sedge warblers, *9*
shearwaters, *11*
  short-tailed, *18*
  slender-billed, *19*
sheep, blue, *21*
snails, *26, 27*
songbirds, *18*
squid, *11*
swallows, *5, 7, 8, 9, 18*
swifts, *16*
tags, marker, *7*
taiga, *20, 30*
transhumance, *21, 30*
tundra, *4, 20, 30*
turtles, green, *17*
wading birds, *18*
warblers, *18*
wasps, *14*
waxwings, *10, 11*
whales, *6, 9, 12, 22, 23, 29*
  blue, *22*
  gray, *6, 23*
  humpback, *23*
white bass, *15*
whitefish, *24*
white stork, *18*
wildebeests, *8, 20*
wolves, *20–21*
zebras, *8, 9*